EMBODIED ENCIRCLED - AN EVERLASTING CYCLE

RAJ DARJI

Thank you, self-doubt.

This book would not be possible without you.

Contents

Contents

Preface

Dear Reader,

Thank you so much for buying my book.

'Embodied Encircled – An Everlasting Cycle' is my 2nd poetry book, consisting of several poems, each conveying a distinct story we encounter at different phases of our life.

The several emotions we feel in this roller-coaster journey. Sometimes overjoyed, sometimes overburdened and we overcome every obstacle which comes across on our path.

I have tried my best to recite and convey the story as well as emotion through my poems. I hope you connect with my book and it cements some space in your memory. The poems are really close to me and I am optimistic that they will strike a special chord with you too.

I wish you have a beautiful time reading.

Regards,

Raj Darji

Acknowledgements

'Embodied Encircled - An Everlasting Cycle' my book would not be possible without the support of many of people in my life.

I would like to thank my family who stood by me each step of my way. Their faith helped me keep working on my craft. The amount of strength they provided to my wings played a crucial role in my flight.

My friends who acted as the biggest driving force in this journey. They were the first one's who read my poem and stories. They critiqued me the best way possible.

My school teachers who guided me in my frame of work, they went through it and enhanced my writing skills. A dear thanks to 'Creative Writing Modern Age (CWMA)' group where I met a lot of writers across the globe. I shared my work and gained a lot of knowledge.

A special thanks to Ian Beckley for the cover photo which I availed through the 'Pexel App'.

Lastly, the entire team of 'Notion Press Publishers' I will always be grateful to you. Thank you for the trust you displayed in my book. You made the journey of publishing of my book truly amazing.

Thank you so much everyone!

Prologue

Our life is surrounded by various stories of which we are a part in some way and there are many people who become part of our story. Humans existence is dependent on other members of the society, who contribute in different shape and form to our life. We are interlinked to one-another, playing our part in each other's storyline.

We embody one story. The story of our life where each passing day we meet new people. We progress towards our destination and with each step we account new memories. Some steps help us move forward while some do pull us back, making it difficult to move ahead. Sometimes we are all alone to fight but there are instances when someone approaches their hand in order to support, writing a new chapter.

We are encircled by numerous people, innumerable stories. Our discourse with one another bridges connection, creating a society of individuals having a common faith, belief and aim. We strive together on these journey, embarking on different routes interconnecting, ending up into a bewildering puzzle. Still we keep trying to figure out a way leading to open road.

The stories we discover ranges from self-doubt, love, depression, uncertainty, complex relations and fight with one self. The struggle with different aspects of life makes it difficult to stand strong and hold every segment firmly. The grip keeps weakening and the fear that everything will fall continue to rise.

The progression of a day and the arrival of night brings a lot of things for one to cater. From the need to mold ourselves under the sunlight, the task of acting gets difficult with presence of dusk and the urge to escape this situation grow tenfold. The only time one can truly find peace is the advent of night. As the world submerges down the horizon, there is nothing left to consider apart from oneself.

The cycle of life keeps flowing without any interval. Its circulation is infinite with no end. Yet undefined in so many ways.

To Rise

1. Everyday

Every day I wake up, I hope – today will be better than yesterday,
I walk ahead in that path to outshine and ignite my true potential,
To uphold my promises in this world filled with potholes,
I instruct myself to be determined whenever I crossroads,
With a passage of meaningless words and sentences:
I try to reframe and derive some sense in my pointless life.
Most days I am left with disappointment and self-doubt,
In agony I retaliate by self-harm; I disorganize my mental state - I hate myself,
There are moments of complete grief when I can't even cry,
Or deny my faults, I wonder obscure like a broken stone,
Impalpable emotions run though my veins – in vain – with no definite reason to breathe,
I end up looking like a wanderer, unaware of his forthcoming after all the hardship.
Some days I am taken by surprise, somehow they are better than the rest,
Not because they are perfect, it is just about that desire to live I possess,
Though haphazard, I prospect to see the better half – neglecting the other side like hypothetical part,

Perpetually inhabiting a false life to forget unforgiving scares,
They keep reinventing themselves to confirm their place,
Uninformed by my surrounding I continue to walk clueless.

2. I Don't Know

I don't know why I smile?
Every time I walk into the day light,
Between many faces surrounding,
It has turned into a necessity for life.

I don't know why I hold my tears?
In this weird world where everyone just exist,
I am unable to see life maybe I am blind,
Or it is just the way we live and humans reside.

I don't know why I lie every time?
That I am happy however stuck in quest,
Where my life is a mystery to my own self,
A healthy surrounding to grow, I manifest.

I don't know why I have to act fake?
There are moments I feel loss of individuality,
My perspective are mere words in this rush,
There are mirrors visible without peculiarity.

I don't know why am I living?
To fulfil my wishes and desires before I die,
Willing to achieve dreams and satisfy my soul,
While I just compensate every second I breathe.

3. Deceptive

Smiles are deceptive,
Because they lead to perspective,
About a person,
Unknown of his suffering…

His turbulence to crisis,
The burden not measured by size,
Price to his life,
Unsold to happiness, devastated by time…

Blossoming flowers,
Changing season, unending sorrow,
Claustrophobic to crowd,
Staying alone bridging vicinity to soul…

A lot of molding,
He serves himself with scolding,
To do as people say,
And keep that smile intact to his face…

It's tough to convert coal into diamond,
And a life wishing peace turning cold,
No more hold over things,
Nothing left to unfold with misery at my door…

I close the curtains,
To find darkness away from the shine,
A corner to cry,
Making a way for tears before I put again that smile…

4. Tell Me

Tell me, why can't I cry? Being a man or a boy,
Because that doesn't make me, an emotionless toy,
For everyone to play around and make me annoy,
With words tuning strong and stern, I better don't be rough,
To my own self or dear one's, surrounding my neck with cough,
Whether I should be patient or impulsive with my actions? It's tough.

Tell me, why can't I be myself? It's okay if you find me different,
Willingly they assume-accuse, I give my reasons, still I am incoherent,
My choices are questioned and answers they demand, but never considerate,
Personalities alike in the crowd are accepted with delight,
Unaccepting change and nature they can't define, we are left deprive,
Stumbling from one end to another, I am losing my own sight.

Tell me, why can't I fail? Isn't it a part of everyone's life,
We all go through bad times, when things aren't working, we strife,
The conflict arises within, we start losing hope, unable to stay alive,
We want someone to support and help us in those moments,
To combat that rough patch, to surpass and restart with content,
To end up victorious this time, for ages to remember and respect.

5. Quest

I close my eyes and can see my life,
It is absurd how I wish for light staying submerge in dark,
Alone I whisper, I talk to connects the dots,
Few anecdotes, I create in dreams.
I scream to be heard but patiently turn into a listener,
It feels like a prisoner, without any reason suffering
punishment just because of contradiction,
I imagine fictional tales in relation to the way,
I want to live,
Practically suffering with whatever is arriving at my
door-step,
Preparing myself for victory, I only conquer dust,
It's tough, it is; you may believe or not,
It's not your fault, if you don't!
You only saw my shoes,
You never walked.
I don't see labels to my face when moonlight comes into
place,
It makes me surrender the task of acting,
In command of people's judgments and thoughts,
What is right and wrong? According to them,
Where I feel no home or freedom to uphold my trueness,
Which has now turned into a quest?

6. It's Fictional

Just hold me in your arms, before I try to create,
Any more distance between both of us,
I don't wish to spend another year just dreaming:
Of us being together, rather I want to be with you.

I am getting rid of my horrible humor and boredom,
In an attempt, to see you smile, to never make you cry,
Then rest my head on your shoulder and enjoy the best of time,
I'll try whatever I can to make it last till the rest of our life.

However, I can only emphasize how much I love you,
And cannot truly confide to you what it means to me,
We are two parallel lines, never meant to intersect at any stage,
Though, we met - an accident – I guess, I need to forget.

Somehow, I am unable to act on my words,
Moving on, maybe simple when you have memories -
To cherish, but I stay deserted of this luxury,

Away from you and I don't plan to come close.

❧❧❧

I know this poem won't reach to you still I continue to hope,
If it does and you tend to ask, 'For whom, you wrote that poem?'
Even if I want to step up and disclose, the fear of losing you will stop me,
I won't be honest and would probably say: 'It's fictional.'

7. Tenderness

My sensitivity was surrounded by questions,
Thousands of faces, hundreds of threads,
Entangled among each other created a mess,
Thoughts and emotions I suppressed with regret of my actions,
People didn't consider anything not even a fraction,
They kept asking, to push my feelings inside,
For a second, I was convinced to kill them dead,
I tried my best but they stayed alive because of my affection.

I left everyone behind and started thinking about myself,
People found me selfish while I was just giving importance,
To things which I prioritize and find necessary to resolve,
In order to accept and work on my life to enhance,
My overall living whereas keeping in mind I nurture self-love,
I wish our society becomes more open to tenderness.

8. Questioning Myself

I am asking my reflection, 'Are you a good person?',
I receive silence in response, enforce of agitation,
Conquest by life in stake of imprison - this situation,
Failing to find destination and ever binding reservation.

Most times I wish to help others however lack sense,
'How truly can I help?' unsettled I place myself at rest:
I continue interrogating infertile land and infuriating fact -
It keeps showcasing mirror, an identity of my true self.

I haven't slept since past few nights in dark blue light,
My harmful strides nurturing one heartless life,
'Do you have any emotions?' I feel numb by reply,
In arrest of expectations - I cannot recall when I last cried.

Unworthy I guess for any sort of help or happiness,
I wander from one stop to another for solutions,
To fill gaps with myself but I only conquer emptiness,
Death over life, questioning myself: 'Do you have any answers?'

9. Reasons

Why everyone wants reason for everything?
When they can't hear the truth,
Which is just another form of perspective,
With various shades from different angles.
Meanwhile everybody wants to speak,
And scream, 'There are hardly any listeners!'
The reason behind calling this situation – An Irony,
Is maybe because it has power to fire the tension.
My mind is trying the figure the next line now,
Since the first eight hardly connects or make sense,
And if someone questions, to my defense I would say:
'They are just as meaningless as most of our lives.'
Probably this is where the poem should end,
But there are words revolting in my head,
Trying to find a place and ensure their existence,
However, they will make me repeat my previous thoughts.
Almost every time I write the same thing,
And today when I sat to write something different,
I ended up writing the above lines becoming -
One of the smartest poem written by me, which is completely pointless.

10. Empty Room, Closed Door

Empty room, closed door,
Vacant space and my lost hope,
Accompanying my unfulfilled dreams,
Turned into scary epilates, I scream.

I am fond of and urge for silence,
But I fear it's undying existence,
Quite faithful to a nobody,
Like me, who is surrounded by agony.

I sit in solitude awaiting storm,
To destruct and defeat human norms,
Harmful to freedom, binding shackles,
Restricting my flight impending feathers.

The walls around me are evident of that,
Preventing my growth an irrefutable fact,
I don't see an escape or any opening,
Maybe I am blind to see my forthcoming.

Why do I feel secure being arrested?
Rather than damaged or throbbed,
I somehow found a mechanism to survive -
Keep breathing; it's okay if you aren't alive.

11. Will Everything be Fine?

Questions are a part of life until you have answers for them,
Once silence replaces and finds existence it becomes a daunting circle,
Which keeps repeating, horrifying its place in our living,
Inevitable circumstances cuddling and reinforcing fear,
Where tears, being fragile couldn't hold themselves back,
Unfortunate or foolish I don't know how to describe that phase?
My everyday presence had lost its senses,
Failure was more than just a constant thing,
Unable to act or process, I was losing that little courage I did possess,
Somewhere, it had vanished and the reasons were unknown,
My failures had a hand in it but the real suspect,
I felt was someone else.

I didn't know whether I was alone or I had isolated myself,
To run away from that situation, those faces who believed me,
Who showed faith in me and I had broken that!
I hated myself for everything going on,
It was depressing and unforgiving for me,

The way I was cursing others for my faults,
I didn't hold my composure even when I knew things were not going,
The same manner I assumed when I started,
I was weak to accept my weaknesses; I kept trying and wasting everyone's effort,
I feared failure and confiding my wrong decision,
I held on to it, hoping for a change, until there was no way ahead,
I fall from the narrow edge I was standing; with my entire life to repent.

I formed shackles around myself and became lifeless,
My strength to complete the quest had vanished,
The oath and those words I said to make everyone believe now felt worthless,
I was unforgiving to myself but life had to move on,
Even I had to; but never did I imagine failing however I failed,
With no 2nd plans clueless, I couldn't accept the reality and plan further,
Turning stationary physically, mentally and emotionally,
I didn't cry wanted to, I thought I shouldn't waste them for my selfish reason.

Time passed, leaving behind scares,
Ultimately I went on different path where life took me,
Now whenever I look back things do make sense to the slightest,
I have changed and evolved to a better version of myself,
My perspective have formed new shapes they differ a lot from the past,
I speak less, I breathe more, I have to live, I dare to lose,
I don't dream anymore, I just work,
Trying to answer one question,
'Will Everything Be Fine?'

Regardless of Dusk

12. Predicament

In this world, there are no boundaries or differences,
Except for the ones we make for ourselves,
Which we draw to withdraw ourselves from damage,
Or engage in materialistic escape – harmful, addictive and lacks resistance,
Overpowering in fashion of relief, sculpturing an infamous tale,
Predicament of worldly gaze, surrounded by haste,
I cast myself in such situations to not feel safe,
I force myself to suffer and challenge to chase,
Unrealistic expectations, far beyond my sphere,
In order to overturn several limitation people have framed,
To go beyond them, conquering my fears and create,
A memorable landscape and phantom my existence,
Still be remembered and admired by people,
Not many though, only the ones who truly matter.

13. Myopia

I am suffering from myopia,
Things coming from a distance appear blur to my eyes,
I don't know how to channelize my thoughts?
Put them into action and bear results.
I just wander, not getting involved in candid conversations,
My dear one's are scared,
They question me, 'Do I have any sight?'
I stay quiet, frightened in my own delusionary mind.
Walking on my path of life,
I see roads getting diverged asking me to make choice, take decision,
I show them my back,
Fear of being called a loser, I lack anticipation.
Unable to define or memorize,
Filled with excuses to support my counter in response,
I haven't found a purpose,
The truth which hides between this lines.
Maybe spectacles can help me find a vision,
To draw my life more colorful apart from black and white,
Since we, humans are grey; mostly work like ashtrays,
I am finding a way out of this place, taking me to the source of light.

14. Sweet Sad Story

I have a sweet sad story for you to remember,
This world exists on love if you have ever ponder,
We communicate it mostly through our simple gestures,
Our affection and care stays with that person forever.

I have fallen in love but could never truly express,
Every time I found a reason to keep them suppress,
Hesitant to even start that conversation I stayed at a distance,
Being her good friend, I was happy just by her presence.

We used to talk a lot and I feared to say something unwanted,
Though with time I learned to mend my words and pretend,
She never had a hint however my friends got a hold,
They kept asking me in order to confirm yet I didn't disclose.

I was adamant to keep her out of this emotional mess,
Our friendship was precious to me than anything else,
However, destiny had some different plans for us,
One day she suddenly asked me to meet at a place.

She was anxious sitting in front of me unlike her behavior,
A positive, happy person and was always ready to endeavor,
'Do you like me?' She asked and my face couldn't cover,
Sadly, what I felt for her was easily visible, I hid in silence further.

She told me her reasons, I was listening to her quietly,
'I don't think I can be in a relationship.' She managed to say;
She was ambitious and had many dreams which I knew,
I smiled brightly, she got to know I withstand her that way.

Thankfully, we continue to be friends even today with delight,
Our dynamic has not changed at all, the most beautiful sight.

15. I Love You, I Truly Do!

Our love story is nothing short of a Bollywood movie,
The time we first met it wasn't expected, informed or planned,
Which made me furious honestly because I am not a fan of surprises,
That instantly made me disconnect from you,
Also you were not much affable or tried to comfort me.

Being an introvert the coldness between us did not delight me,
It made me self-analyze whether I was acting in a wrong way to someone?
I ended up realizing I should try to break the ice and rectify the situation,
Sadly, I faltered in my attempts resulting in complete mess,
The only thing I wanted next was not to see you anywhere around.

My life enjoys to see me in stress hence I couldn't escape your presence,
You were around me every moment and I was disgusted without a reason,

I don't like changes and having you was a big change for me,
Slowly I was able to gel with you, I found peace when things started to sort,
We spent time getting to know each other and I apologize for the way I treated you.

Gradually, I have started cherishing your company, you accepted me as I am,
You did not wish to change instead you helped me to love myself more,
I have kept you aware of all my flaws and every time I do so you start making me count,
'Why I should get rid of you soon as possible?' because you don't believe,
Someone else will take your existence gracefully and might be an issue for me.

However, I wish to reassure, 'You are the best thing happened to me.'
And today I want you to know; I Love You, I Truly Do – Stretchmarks!

16. The Parents Lost Their Child

He was sweating every day and night, tears were crying from his eyes,
His hands were fumbling and feet trembling,
He was losing control over his body,
But he needed to fight with his lust for drugs driving inside him,
Killing him those four walls alone in which he was isolated,
He was dying trying to remember what pushed him into this hell?
His failures, his faults, where he couldn't decipher what is right and what is wrong?
He didn't pause to overlook his mistakes and find a way from his unwanted destination,
He arrived at the stage of repent.
His parents were noticing the changes in his behavior,
They tried to talk to him in order to understand the matter,
But he denied acting rebellion, he feared being tagged weak, who is unable to handle his own grief,
He was walking on a steeper lane, aware that he is going to fall,
But, he didn't take help instead got involved in drugs,
An associate for him to get relief from his pain,

A ride to the fairy tale land away from the shower, the rain of sorrow in which he was drowning,
Still, nothing changed apart from the water.

Addiction ignited and intensified his unabashed melancholy,
Unapologetically intoxicated and separated from real world,
His cruel life swinging with the wind carrying the scent of medicines,
He had lost all his senses in grooved with pills, his hands filled with injection marks,
His parents came to know about him, they were left in turmoil,
Questioning their parenting; wanting to know, 'Where did we go wrong?'
Decided to take the situation in hold, taking their son away from this,
A tough exterior they presented; though broken interiorly.

They took him to medication hoping their son gets rid of his addiction,
He wished for the same, when he paused and recollected his sense,
He pressed himself away from the person he had become,
And was recalling his forgotten self, who was passionate and ambitious, positive and victorious,

Unfortunately, never failed and didn't know how to react when he faced,
He commenced a new way to life, but every deed has his prize and repercussion for life,
Drugs had barely left anything inside him and his body turned cold,
He died. The Parents lost their child.

17. Please do remember

Please do remember:
Even if you don't believe me,
Trust me, I believe you.

Passing time may create differences,
You might find a need to bring distance,
To gather jumbled words,
To precisely carve finer curves.

I would be hesitant at first,
But then I will agree and respect –
Your decision to comprehend,
Things running out of our hand.

Please do remember:
Even if you don't believe me,
Trust me, I believe you.

Our conversations will turn short,

It might become difficult to meet,
To reach any clarity of our pact,
With each day concluding its depth.

I fear we'll get separated,
No longer we would see,
Our shadows walking together,
And those street will again be empty.

Please do remember:
Even if you don't believe me,
Trust me, I believe you.

My faith might do more harm,
Than good when - you would be ready,
To get detached from what we share,
And you find it difficult to communicate.

Tell me whatever is running in your head,
Try to bear my ridiculous behavior,
I won't cross any limits, if I do -
Hear me apologize but never forgive.

Please do remember:
Even if you don't believe me,
Trust me, I believe you,
And that's never going to change.

Just a request before we end,
Let us dance on our favorite song,
If things don't take a dramatic tone,
Final few intimate moments.

A bit awkward in each other's arm,
Imperfect movements enduring our dance,
Gently holding and moving away,
Entering into our new solitude world.

Please do remember:
Nothing about me,
If it stops you from moving on,
Towards a better and happy life.

18. Mirage

If life was honest, we all might have lack water in our eyes,
No simile or metaphor to define the pain and suffering,
We must be filled with acceptance and passion to strive,
Efforts and resilience being the words to define success.

Wisdom has its own flaws with no cure, visible to only few,
You can't make everyone happy with your knowledge you understand,
And leave people disappointed by restricting them to do,
By predicting, atrocities which may arise with the situation in hand.

Adjustment is a white canvas can accommodate various colors,
While you soon realize how it depicts your life by turning black,
You aren't living just comprehending by fitting in the required attire,
Seeking happiness in others smile - a satire labelled to your act.

Summing up what is good and bad? I found nothing true,
However I can conclude life is a big mirage we draw.

19. He Without You...

Why am I surrendered to you?
Life feels incomplete though when were we together?
For you to remember me,
I question myself, 'Do I even matter?'
Is it better to move on…
But the memories we created as friends,
Which led to my emotions for you,
I smile reading these lines over my foolishness.

Distance between us has been prevalent,
I don't even recall the last time we met,
However, I am unable to forget the fights we had,
Our school days, when you were rebellious,
And most of the times I was quite,
I won't say 'I was nice!' I had my mischievous side,
Of which very few were aware of and you were one them,
Those were my little pleasures,
And one of them was secretly looking at you.

The next we meet I wish to confess,
And I hope you accept me with my flaws,

I may not be the best suited for you,
Still I want us to be together,
I imagine you making me the best version of myself,
Nothing larger than life; just a simple love story we have,
I mingle these words creating a special tune,
For a beautiful lady and that's you.

But the truth won't change,
That you are very close to me,
And yet too far not even visible to my eyes,
Without you it's difficult to frame the perfect picture of life.

20. She Without You...

Why my life is deserted without him?
We talk daily about a lot of things,
Unfortunately, not in reality,
Every conversation is fantasized just in my head,
I have his number but it's been a while since we last talked,
Ages when we last met and with my sudden call,
I don't want to turn things into a mess,
I know he loves me and both of us lack communication skills.

I try to understand this silence between us,
The distance we have created and unrest it has caused,
Of course, we can resolve it,
But then we both are waiting for the other person,
To take the first step in this fairy tale,
It's magical how we connect with so ease,
Still fall short to express,
This silence is depressing with the flow of life.

Does that moment of truth will ever come?
Or maybe it's time to make that moment happen,
Should I call and confide everything?

How will he react? How should I respond?
Is this a good idea to confess on a call?
With lots of question, I lost my confidence,
And welcomed self-doubt in my empty mind,
I am clueless regarding our destiny.

I think I need to stop thinking about him,
That's the only way left for me,
If nothing I'll be happy I took a decision,
But will I really be happy? I question myself.

21. A Friend

I have a friend and we are pretty alike,
We believe strongly in love,
Also escape from its existence in our life,
We aren't made for it we assume.

I have a friend more of a replica,
As we walk happily with our belly,
We eat without showing any mercy,
Only one life in hand we avoid doing tally.

I have a friend and we resemble a lot,
The worst of jokes which never fall short,
To irritate everyone around,
We laugh hysterically with no control.

I have a friend quite similar to me,
We are afraid to talk and single,
Find socializing extremely difficult,
We feel it's better to stay at home.

I have a friend officially my mirror,
We have many friends! but a slight error –
Nobody around us all in our imagination,
We are our best friends happy with ourselves.

22. Home - Family

Tired of everything in his life and work place,
He travels back to home,
With questions in his head leading to frustration,
A battle he fights inside which keeps on increasing,
With each passing day and nobody finds a trace,
His blissful face hides a thousand scares he carries with himself,
Trying to keep all threads attached,
He splits to each end in order to keep them in touch,
Their happiness, their necessities, their goodwill,
He forgot thinking about himself a long back,
And lives with regret somehow making peace with it,
He enters his home and his kids come running towards him,
They are smiling seeing him return,
Bringing life to his life,
He forgets all his stress and starts playing with them,
His better half gives him a hug and they kiss,
'How was your day?' She asks him,
'It was empty and now it's complete!' He quotes,
At night, the moment he closes his eyes,
He relives all those smiles he brought,
And goes to sleep without any burden.

Uphold Till The End

23. Only if...

Only if you remember me, do suggest –
'How can I erase someone's memory?'
Someone, I desire I had more memories to cherish,
Or belief in love to confide my earnest feelings…
I thought to restrict them with me,
Would be in best of interest for both of us.
Sorry, I took decision on your behalf as well,
But I don't think the scheme of things could have been much different,
Even if there was any possibility I'll stay clueless,
Either ways it contributed to my section of regret,
Still I am happy, wherever and whoever, we are today,
At least, we don't try to escape each other's eyes.
You don't have to overthink before agreeing,
To any plan created by our common friends,
You feel comfortable to take me out for parties,
Where you are left alone and I am your companion,
You even talk about him at several instances,
I want you to stop while I play my part as a good friend.
I wish to disconnect from the connect I have with you,
It would be simpler only if we had anything to part ways.

24. …you knew the story from my end

Enlighten him that I have the same questions,
The same urge, to express my love,
But he kept building bridges – not leaving space for me,
To confess; I was feeling arrested by my own emotions,
I could not allow them to be free,
Hence they forever stayed with me.
You did your best in order to hide how you truly felt…
Though you never realized by your several action I got hurt,
I had nothing to support that you might feel the same,
Until I was with someone else,
I could see everything – you were broken,
Still you managed to hold a smile and contact with my eyes.
I never think twice before agreeing to any plan,
Because I know hardly anyone cares for you,
You stay there with me during parties, we both want to escape,
Just as you hate to accept the fact that you are alone,
I sometimes intentionally talk about him with you,
So that you can understand and move on in life.
It is tough for me to easily disconnect with you,
I just hope someday you see our story from my end.

25. Failed

Let the world know I am a failure,
And allow me free from all worldly barriers,
In trenches I have been living forever,
Unable to go beyond my unending fears.

Everyone has ruled over my life,
Apart from me and my discarded beliefs,
Overruled by expectations price,
Like a disease – killing me from inside.

Traumatized by insecurities and crisis,
Arriving at multiple intervals, holding my rise,
Above darkness to welcome light,
In a setting not acquired by fright.

I corner myself without any thought,
Then wander around for water in drought,
To achieve what I want, I fought,
But helpless in slave of my weaknesses, I lost.

I am thankful to both silence and noise,
Gathered around my defeat – scattered voice,
Having blur faces, I couldn't read one,
I sat quietly in vicinity of my soul all alone.

I have innumerable questions to be asked,
Who truly failed? Me or the society at large.

26. A Perfect Blend

Art is a perfect blend of imagination and reality,
A mechanism to enable transcendence,
Away from the quest of life,
To energize – true sense of liveliness,
Not far from the rest, being a part of the mess,
Addressing escape from imprisonment,
Allowance to create and regulate, not just follow:
Unjust worldly path which may lead you to the end,
Bringing nothing at your door but leaving you with repent,
And to fix that dent is when art comes into picture,
To prevent any more harm, to cure past scares,
To commence a new start, to attain peace,
However not under a flask of delusion.
It offers substance to fulfillment ahead of any ailment,
For you to surrender your thoughts on a blank page.

27. Devotional Magic

An over whelming rush of emotions,
Transpiring an individual to a better world,
One can hardly explain that sensation,
Still wish for it to be duly present forever.

It might not be visible to our naked eyes,
But it's presence can lift even a dead soul,
The uncanny potential or magic it persists,
Does work in silence and fragrance life.

It has devotional attributes, sparkling light,
To disappear darkness surrounded by,
Someone's existence, imparting fright,
Gets replaced with smile - resembling peace.

Some momentary escape from reality,
Engaged in cruelty, we emphasize on creating:
An improved picture functioning primarily,
For ourselves, walking on the half edge.

Beyond excellence or perfection, it is pure,
Not ruled by materialistic dominance,
It nurtures living in truest form, displaying care -
For humans, overlooking any barrier.

The sense of transcendent feeling is a bliss,
Cruel patches of time get stuffed with love,
Immense strength to endure it possesses,
To recover, evolve and fly in the open sky.

28. Thank you!

We are walking together finally after years,
Of distance adjoining our existence,
We found each other's presence to nurture,
The love, we have been hiding inside us.

I could never imagine it would be this magical,
To be with you in solitude at one place,
This phase of breath, makes me feel grateful,
To life, ignoring the time, I have spent alone.

I wonder what helped us to stay connected,
Even when we were in distinct corners –
Of this world, with no source to get in contact,
Each day we kept thinking of one another.

The drought of physical touch and comfort,
We experienced for a prolonged period,
The importance of care and support, it taught,
We continue to hold on until we are dead.

I am happy you are sitting right by my side,
As I complete writing this poem about us,
I would like to thank you for being with we,
Despite of knowing my every single flaws.

29. Walking. Understanding. Realizing

I am walking with the moonlight,
Talking to him about my daily fights,
I barely ask him 'Is he doing alright?'
And I notice how selfish is man-kind,
Who likes to speak and wish to be heard,
Figuring out the seed of greed in our breed,
I hardly agree that humans can affiliate,
If we could it would have been great relief.

I wish to know the concept of supremacy,
Thinking about its place in our life daily,
Not sure but I am understanding it slowly,
How irrelevant and of no importance it is,
The concept of being unworldly is a bliss,
No change or unnecessary molding to fix,
In this society entirely free to breathe,
And live a life with peace away from the race.

Realizing the true happiness lies in smile,
Just do what your heart feels and fly,

Discovering infinite possibilities in life,
While it create huddles making us resilient,
Staying true to our work and being obedient,
Submissive to hard work practicing patience,
Also, giving rest to our mind to process better,
No recipe for success just need to act clever.

30. Fly

Anonymous people synonymous question they ask,
Disturbing me; it feels suffocating being in this flask.

Lifeless in void of pleasure, avoided by bliss,
In search of my vicinity people found me foolish.

Convenient to others my inconvenience with failures,
Submissive to hard work though useless as per culture.

Dormant in prison of thousand speculations,
People don't find my craft worthy of occupation.

Still with conviction over my art I write,
Forming two sections of my life what is wrong? What is right?

My life finds breathe I am able to handle situation with ease,
I dive in delusion with my mind finding peace.

I want someone to be around with me,
But then I think it's better to suffer alone let the rest be free.

I enjoy the fast flowing wind strengthening my wings,
I assume they are ready to fly crossing all obstacles time brings.

31. Alive & Breathing

Living for myself, people assume betrayal,
To the real world where tears should not shed even at worse,
Being a mere human is tough hence we have turned into animal,
Where everyone waits for an opportunity to get rid of others.

Each individual possesses their distinct individuality,
Difficult to accept; we are asked to paint ourselves black or white,
Nobody admits the fact that most humans are grey,
I continue to live my life, truly a lie, under the bright sunlight.

I whisper unable to raise my voice, maybe not confident enough,
To withstand my thoughts; I hide them to suffer no loss,
Of the one's I love and are dear to me, I am becoming that stuff -
I fear to be; in this hopeless world I am in search of hope.

Though I exist and breathe, I hardly sense my presence,
Every day in life, is like service to society, to amend I am not apart,
I barely succeed in my task as people keep their eyes on me,
But the moment I let my words fall free I find no need to be a part.

I fear darkness while moonlight is my dear friend,
Away from the day every time being surrounded by human rush,
I hear silence screaming unable to bear and clutch at the end,
Freedom to be myself, there are no more eyes looking for its ash.

The immorality submerges down the horizon after sunset,
Presenting a wide black sky for stars to confide their place,
Arising aspiration as I stare at them for hours without being afraid,
Walking slowly, passing through air, I cherish life – a borderline quest.

Unfulfilled dreams ignite at night to accompany they sit by my side,

I realize how silly, weird with no purpose yet elegant they were,
We re-unite and talk about those plans we could never execute,
I have buried them inside my coffin long back, still they are alive.

I sense happiness as I continue to draw my life,
However momentary, it is worthy to live when I hold pen in hand,
A blank page, my empty life and words fill them with substance,
My persona shines brightly as I smile with content, just not to pretend.

32. Eyes Turned Blind

The night is so beautiful with silence spread far and wide,
A tide of thoughts arising in my mind and in absence of light I hide,
Words inside my soul, buried and repressed, thunders by my side,
I fight to find my true identity acquainted by sorrow, left hostile.

❧❧❧

I am having conversations with myself trying to figure my life,
Urging for answers of unanswered questions and sphere of lies,
Which surrounds me, fears me that I don't have wings to fly,
And to surpass, breaking thresholds I have created around myself.

❧❧❧

I wish to be a butterfly in a setting bursting flower fragrance,
Incorporated with space where I can discover my presence,
To grow and soar, in vicinity of nature and it's enriching essence,
I can somewhere be this way for moments only in darkness.

In my existence I reside, the moonlight makes me alive,
Away from this world which is harsh and where I am deprived,
I spend time in thinking of the medicines I should prescribe,
My own self to find relief or simply this situation I should imbibe.

Half the night has passed and my sleep leaving me behind,
I have been sitting the entire time thinking about my life undermined,
Reckoning in regards to everyone's happiness my effort to be combined,
As it came to my priorities and eyes turned blind.

33. Death

I fear the end called death,
Precisely, It's inevitable existence,
Which is invisible to our sight,
Accompanied by some dreadful experience.
There is no option for us to skip,
We cannot escape any hurdle,
Making sure we do not let our life slip,
Holding it firmly, need to move further.
Uncertainty present everywhere,
Surrounding us, we act restless,
In fear of ending up nowhere,
We get thrust into a wrong place.
Unwelcomed and unaware of its arrival,
We continue fighting our own battle.

About The Author

Raj Darji is a budding writer, poet, blogger and a student. He is 17 years old and writing is his prime medium to communicate. He is the author of the poetry book, 'Walking Through Shades – In Search of Light'. Also, he has been co-author of 5 anthology books. He is select writer of 'Split Poetry India'. 'One of You' is the name of his writing page on Instagram. 'Gush of Thoughts' is the name of his blogger page. He is from Mumbai and pursuing studies in the stream of Arts. Connect with him:

Email Id - imrd54321@gmail.com

Instagram - @_one.of.you

A new journey commences...

9 798886 671148

Printed by Libri Plureos GmbH in Hamburg, Germany